D1038696

*This book is lovingly dedicated to Jim Eaton, whose death in 1968 brought me my greatest pain, but led me to my life's most rewarding work . . . helping others in grief.*

# GRIEF

## A Natural
## Reaction
## to Loss

*Second Edition*

Marge Eaton Heegaard

FAIRVIEW PRESS, MINNEAPOLIS

GRIEF: A NATURAL REACTION TO LOSS, SECOND EDITION © 2002 Marge Eaton Heegaard. All rights reserved. No part of this publication may be used or reproduced in any manner whatsoever without written permission, except in the case of brief quotations embodied in critical articles and reviews. For further information, please contact the publisher.

Published by Fairview Press, 2450 Riverside Avenue, Minneapolis, Minnesota 55454. Fairview Press is a division of Fairview Health Services, a community-focused health system providing a complete range of services, from the prevention of illness and injury to care for the most complex medical conditions.

*Library of Congress Cataloging-in-Publication Data*

Heegaard, Marge Eaton.
    Grief : a natural reaction to loss / Marge Eaton Heegaard.--2nd ed.
        p. cm.
    Includes bibliographical references.
    ISBN 1-57749-112-2 (pbk. : alk. paper)
        1. Grief. 2. Bereavement--Psychological aspects. 3. Loss (Psychology) I. Title.

    BF575.G7+
    155.9--dc21                                                2001055612

First Edition: 1994
Second Edition: 2002

Printed in Canada
05        04        03        02                    5        4        3        2        1

Cover design by Laurie Ingram
Interior design by Timothy W. Larson
Acknowledgments for previously published work on page 90.

**Disclaimer**
This publication is designed to provide accurate and authoritative information in regard to the subject matter covered. It is sold with the understanding that the publisher is not engaged in the provision or practice of professional mental health advice or services. If advice or other professional assistance is required, the services of a qualified and competent professional should be sought. Fairview Press is not responsible or liable, directly or indirectly, for any form of damages whatsoever resulting from the use (or misuse) of information contained in or implied by these documents.

For a free current catalog of Fairview Press titles, please call toll-free 1-800-544-8207, or visit our Web site at www.fairviewpress.org.

# CONTENTS

*Introduction*                                                     1

ACCEPTING LOSS AND CHANGE                                          3

RECOGNIZING SOCIAL INFLUENCES ON GRIEF                            9

UNDERSTANDING THE GRIEF PROCESS                                   17

REDUCING FEAR                                                     25

EXPRESSING ANGER IN HEALTHY WAYS                                 31

RESOLVING GUILT                                                   37

MANAGING DEPRESSION                                               45

IDENTIFYING CHILDHOOD LOSSES AND FAMILY ISSUES                   51

SPIRITUALITY                                                      63

COPING WITH STRESS                                                71

CHALLENGING LONELINESS AND FINDING SELF                          79

*Further Reading*                                                87

# GUIDELINES FOR CREATIVE GRIEF WORK

### CREATE A GRIEF JOURNAL

1) Buy a simple three-ring or spiral notebook.
2) Choose a comfortable pen that pleases you.
3) Keep colored pencils, paint, or crayons available to express thoughts and feelings that you cannot express in words.
4) Make time to write each day.
5) Write in a quiet place, or play soft music in the background.
6) Don't worry about spelling, punctuation, or sentence structure.
7) Express your thoughts and feelings honestly.
8) Keep your journal in a safe place, just for you.
9) Reread your journal from time to time to be aware of changes in your behavior and feelings.

### EXPRESS YOURSELF IN POETRY

1) Rhyming isn't necessary. A poem can be a few carefully chosen words arranged in a pleasing form.
2) A lyric poem is one that expresses intense personal emotions.
3) Haiku is a poetic form from Japan. It has three lines, with five syllables in the first line, seven in the second, and five in the third. To create a haiku, use simple words that express a strong feeling and create a vivid image.

### EXPERIMENT WITH ART

1) Allow your inner child to mourn. Use lines, colors, and shapes to express thoughts and feelings too difficult for words.
2) Use a red crayon to scribble and release anger.
3) Use soft blue crayons or watercolors to release sadness.
4) Draw your fears to conquer them.
5) Draw or paint something you enjoy to give yourself a sense of control.

# INTRODUCTION

GRIEF IS THE EMOTIONAL AND BEHAVIORAL REACTION TO LOSS. Though grief is natural and universal, society has taught people to hide their grief. Repressing feelings, however, requires a great deal of energy, and unresolved grief fosters feelings of bitterness and hopelessness.

The loss of a loved one is among the most severe forms of psychological stress. A failure to mourn such a loss can lead to problems with health and relationships. Mourning is the work of grief, the expression of inner feelings. Mourning brings healing.

This book was written to help you understand the dynamics of the grief process and your personal reaction to loss. It encourages mourning, which requires you to recognize and express confusing and painful feelings. It also teaches coping skills to help you move forward as a whole person capable of feeling and experiencing life.

Each chapter includes a number of suggestions for using the creative process to explore feelings and promote self-awareness. Creativity can help you cope with the many difficult emotions, demands, and decisions brought about by your loss. Music, for example, releases painful feelings and brings you comfort and strength. Body movement reduces stress and depression. Painting or drawing provides greater understanding when words cannot describe the enormity of your loss. Writing helps you to recognize and organize your thoughts and feelings.

Bereavement is a time of great loneliness. Even when friends and family members experience the same loss, they grieve in their own way.

The grief work throughout this book will help you discuss and process your emotions with others, fostering a sense of community and reducing your sense of isolation.

For more personal work, begin a journal to record your thoughts and feelings. Your writing will become an important record of your grief work. A journal offers you an opportunity to mourn in a safe, private environment. It can act as a friend or therapist, quietly assisting you in identifying and solving problems. Journaling can help you to integrate your loss, complete any unfinished business, and record the process of your grief work and healing.

Experiment with different creative outlets to discover which is most helpful for you. Take time to renew a forgotten talent or develop a new interest. Your grief journey will be enriched. You will make new discoveries about yourself and move forward as a survivor with unexpected strength and character. Do this for you. You are worth it!

# Accepting
# Loss and Change

"*Mother, they want to translate my book into French.*" *She doesn't answer. Pictures cannot talk, but in a way I think she's smiling. Her picture hangs in my office. She died seven years ago.*

*She died of heart failure in North Dakota while I was in Bangkok— half a world away. I could not be with her as she died. I had wanted to do something special with her for her ninetieth birthday the next month. I will always miss her. I will miss her letters with news of the family. I will miss sharing with her the big and the little events of my life. I lost her memories of the past with her death, but I would always have the gifts of life she gave me.*

*Mother's Day came. I had no mother. I was an orphan. We sold the house that had been there for me for sixty years. My father died in that house seven years earlier, and my grandmother when I was just two.*

*I had truly expected my father to live to be one hundred. The intensity of my grief surprised me when I learned he was terminal, until I gave some thought to all I was losing. He had always been strong and reliable. If I ever needed anything, I knew he was there for me. I lost that sense of security. He also thought I was perfect. No one else ever did or could. I allowed myself to grieve.*

*My parents are gone, but I will always have the greatest gift they gave me . . . the freedom to be myself.*

LOSS IS AN INESCAPABLE PART OF LIVING. Death involves loss and change, and we grieve loss and change. There is no single or easy path for each of us to follow through our grief. There will be risks to take and decisions to make, but each individual must set out on his or her own grief journey to heal and be whole.

Grief is a lonely path. Each loss is as unique as the person and relationship lost. No one else can really understand or tell you what to do. A person's reaction to a death will depend on what the relationship was and how it was lost. The reaction to an untimely, sudden, or violent death will be different than the reaction to a natural and anticipated death. Personal coping skills vary with age, experiences, and needs. Education, family, faith, social groups, and other support systems influence personal reactions to loss.

Major losses create secondary losses. Dreams and expectations are lost along with roles and routines. The death of a child, for example, represents a loss of the future and may be the most intense and long-lasting grief. Parents are expected to be protectors and may feel guilty for failing to prevent their child's death, or they may feel survivors' guilt because children are expected to outlive parents. Secondary losses such as security, control, purpose, independence, pride, trust, faith, and identity may be harder to recognize, but they, too, need to be identified and grieved.

## THE LOSS EXPERIENCE IS PERSONAL

People will grieve similar losses, such as the death of a spouse or partner, in very different ways. For example, a woman's identity is often closely associated with her relationships, so the loss of a partner or child can be experienced as a loss of her own self. Historically, women have been expected to be dependent and to nurture others. They tend to explore feelings, while men tend to seek solutions for problems. Men are often taught to be self-reliant and independent, to have competitive relationships rather than intimate ones. This puts them at a distinct disadvantage, because it is more difficult for them to share feelings. They may try to replace what is lost too quickly in an effort to bring back normal routines, and this can prevent them from fully grieving and healing.

Children often do not begin their grieving until they sense that surviving adults are okay. Grief reactions vary. Because it is difficult for young children to express feelings verbally, their helplessness, frustration, fear, and pain may come out as explosive emotions or destructive, angry behavior rather than tears.

Children often blame themselves for something they did or did not do before their loved one died, or they become angry and blame others. Their behavior will vary from day to day because children are unable to sustain grief. Children need help coping. They must not become "the forgotten grievers," because early loss makes a big impact on their lives.

## THE PATH TO ACCEPTANCE

Grief is a roller coaster of emotions, complete with foreign feelings and a confused sense of self. Grief creates anxiety and insecurity. But the feelings, confusion, and pain are normal and must be experienced in order to reach acceptance and healing.

Grief cannot be ignored, repressed, replaced, refused, or dismissed without severe repercussions. Avoiding the feelings of grief creates problems with health and relationships and will only bring more pain in the future. You must grieve fully and experience the pain to heal and gain personal growth.

Your acute sense of grief will gradually decline in frequency and intensity. You will never forget your loss, but you will gain the ability to recall your loved one without pain. The relationship you shared will always exist in a special place in your heart and in your memories.

Your emotional and social reentry into the everyday world will be gradual, but you will begin to withdraw the emotional energy invested in your loss and reinvest it in new relationships, goals, and activities. You will develop a new sense of self as you weave the loss into your life and begin to live life more fully.

## GRIEF WORK EXERCISES

1) Describe the death and its cause. Was the death sudden or anticipated? Do you have any questions that need to be answered about the death and its cause?

2) Think about how your life has changed since the death. List your major losses and the obvious changes.

3) List your secondary losses. These may be harder to recognize, but there will be many. To help you identify your secondary losses, write out future hopes and dreams that can never be. Include the ways the relationship contributed to your identity, status, prestige, and self-worth.

## JOURNAL

1) Write down memories of your loved one and why the relationship was important to you.

2) Write about the moment you learned of the death. Were you present? If not, how were you told? How did you react?

3) What will you miss most? Identify and list new roles and tasks you will need to learn or will need to find someone else to do.

# RESPONSES TO LOSS

THESE REACTIONS ARE ALL NORMAL and may take as long as two years to pass, but they *will* pass. Check (√) those you experience occasionally and star (*) those you experience often.

## EMOTIONAL RESPONSES

_____ Stunned, dazed, or overwhelmed
_____ Constant thoughts about the deceased
_____ Anxiety because routines have changed
_____ Disbelief or denial of the reality of the death
_____ Feeling vulnerable and unsafe
_____ Sensing, seeing, hearing, or feeling the touch of the deceased
_____ Avoiding personal feelings
_____ Wide mood swings and intense feelings
_____ Feeling abandoned by the one who died
_____ Guilt about things done or not done before the death
_____ More sensitive, angry, or argumentative than usual
_____ Thoughts of self-punishment or suicide
_____ Worries about the health and safety of oneself or others
_____ Thinking no one understands

## BEHAVIORAL AND PHYSICAL RESPONSES

_____ Pain and heaviness in the chest
_____ Keeping overly busy to avoid feeling
_____ Withdrawal from regular activities and friends
_____ Disorganized, restless, forgetful, and confused
_____ Crying at unexpected times and places
_____ Physical complaints and illnesses
_____ Numbness and robotic behavior
_____ Weight loss or gain
_____ Searching for the deceased
_____ Taking care of others rather than self
_____ A need to repeat details of the death
_____ Tightness in the throat
_____ Experiencing symptoms similar to the illness of the deceased
_____ Sleep difficulties and fatigue
_____ Buying things not really needed

# RECOGNIZING SOCIAL INFLUENCES ON GRIEF

The telephone rang early that fall evening, and Dad spoke to someone before he came into the living room.

"Mama has died," he said softly, and returned to his chair and his magazine. He showed no emotion but I knew he was thinking and feeling. He wasn't reading. He wasn't turning pages and the magazine was upside down. I knew he loved his mother greatly, and I remember thinking, "This is what you are supposed to do when someone dies." I was twelve years old.

The father of one of my best friends in high school was a mortician. Our group of friends often met in front of the funeral home after lunch to walk back to school together. We were curious about what was inside. She would let us look at coffins occasionally, but never if there was a body. "You can't go in," she would say emphatically. "There's a body inside."

Years later a neighbor across the street died, and the doctor called me to say his wife would be going over to be with the family and that he hoped I would go, too. I looked across the street and saw the hearse still there. "I can't go," I thought frantically. "The body is there." I went anyway.

Jackie Kennedy . . . no tears . . . so strong with two small children by her side. Her strength steadied an anxious and grief-stricken nation, but many may have learned to deny or conceal personal feelings. Her stoic public image was one I later was to follow.

SOCIETY CAN GREATLY INFLUENCE HOW PEOPLE GRIEVE. Death was once a more anticipated and accepted part of life. In 1900, 53 percent of the world population died before the age of fourteen. Only 17 percent lived past the age of sixty-five. People usually died at home and were buried close to where they lived and worshiped. It was difficult to deny death as part of the life experience.

With advances in medical and scientific technology, it has become easier for us to deny or avoid the realities of death. For some, death may even be viewed as unnatural or a mistake. Many of our family members and friends now die in hospitals and nursing homes. Cemeteries are often distant from the living. Misguided ideas of rugged individualism and unwavering strength discourage and deny the human experience of grief. We may even look to drugs, alcohol, work, or food to medicate or shut out our feelings of grief. We fear death and loss and their resulting pain, so we hide or repress their occurrence. When we do so, we do not heal.

Research has linked problems with physical health to issues of unresolved grief. An acceptance of death, on the other hand, leads us to live life more fully. Running counter to our society's pattern of denial, an emphasis is now being made on understanding and expressing feelings in appropriate ways. For example, the hospice movement is helping families of the terminally ill prepare for, participate in, and come to grips with the death of a loved one. Schools are beginning to recognize behavior and learning problems in grieving young people and provide support and counseling. Even books, television, and theater are beginning to portray death and grief more realistically.

## EXPECTATIONS

Despite advances in grief education, much of society still has unrealistic expectations for bereavement, and grieving people often do not receive adequate information and support. Even some professionals may treat normal reactions to loss as abnormal. We are uncomfortable with grief, so we try to rationalize, repress, and dismiss it. When someone's spouse or partner dies, for example, many people expect grief to last just a few days or weeks, rather than a more realistic two years. And grief often returns with holidays, anniversaries, birthdays, the changing of the seasons, geographic places, and new losses.

Sudden, untimely, or violent deaths often complicate and extend the grief process. Other complicating issues include legal investigations, public notoriety, prolonged resentment, an inability to forgive, not knowing the cause of death, feeling responsible for the death, or feeling relieved because of the death.

## DIFFICULT INTERACTIONS

Those not grieving often do not know how to treat the bereaved. Well-meaning people, for instance, may ask difficult questions or say absurd things to ease your pain. Others may avoid you, say nothing, or talk around the issue, especially if the death was caused by an accident, homicide, suicide, or AIDS. Questions from police, reporters, and medical staff may seem cold and intimidating. It will seem frustrating and unfair, but strive to ask for what you need, express what you do not need, and keep interactions in perspective.

Employers vary greatly in how they treat grieving employees. Most will excuse them for bereavement and time-limited counseling or grief support groups. But some employers may be neither aware nor tolerant of your grief. It is important that you take care of yourself by asking for what you need and expressing your limitations.

## SOCIAL SUPPORT

The grief process is naturally long, and the bereaved often feel isolated in their grief. Some people may turn away from the bereaved out of fear or indifference. But many bereaved people also shut out others so as not to burden them. Everyone needs at least one person to support them and encourage them to grieve. It is important to reach out to others who are present and available to you. Friends who have personally experienced loss can be the most understanding and supportive during your bereavement.

Other support resources are available, too. Religious communities, hospitals, and schools provide support groups where both children and adults can learn about, process, and express their grief in safe, supportive environments. In talking with other grieving people, you can learn coping skills and receive encouragement for personal growth in your grief journey.

With the help of trusted friends, family, and support group members, you will heal from your loss. You will come to let go of the past, accept the present, and move toward investments in your future.

### THINKING

*Thinking back on memories I hold so dear,*
  *I see my visions fading as I add on to the years.*
*Crying through the hard times, smiling through the good,*
  *Holding on to memories is all that I can do.*
*Think of life all over, omitting all the bad,*
  *I try to remember someone by reaching out my hands.*
*Someone grab my hands and hold them tight.*
  *I need love so much right now.*
  *Someone show me light.*

— Joanna Redman, age twelve

# FEELING SHUNNED

*Those whose worlds are still intact cannot understand*
*The agony of being denied future memories.*
*I have become a social leper.*
*To many who look upon my pain,*
*I bring deep fear that it is contagious.*
*They back away and disappear.*

— Lynnette Kay Titus
in loving memory of her son, Ryan

IT IS DISTRESSING WHEN OTHERS AVOID AND SHUN US. No one wants to be a social leper. Those who shy away from us may do so because they don't know how to help us. They may fear that asking about our loved one will just upset us or bring up painful memories. They may think it's easier to be absent or silent than to risk injuring us more.

Most people are not hurtful on purpose. Knowing how to help a bereaved person often takes having been deeply touched by pain. Without this experience, people simply may not know how best to reach out. We must try not to be bitter or resentful.

From *Remembering with Love: Messages of Hope for the First Year of Grieving and Beyond*, by Elizabeth Levang and Sherokee Isle; printed with permission.

## GRIEF WORK EXERCISES

1) List members of your support system. Who can you count on to be a good listener and accept your feelings? Put an asterisk after their names.

2) What images do you recall from books, movies, or TV shows that are related to death or grief?

3) How have clergy, medical personnel, and morticians responded to your loss?

## JOURNAL

1) Write about the different ways society has responded to your loss (include thoughts about your interactions with family, friends, employer, and others).

2) Describe the funeral ritual for your loved one. How was this one different from others you've attended? Who planned it? Was there any family disagreement? Is there anything you wish you had done differently?

3) Are family and friends unable to be as supportive as you would like because of their own grief? What are their losses?

# Understanding
# the Grief Process

Though we had been packing for Jim's twentieth high school reunion, we had to cancel that trip and pack for a trip to the hospital, where Jim would have surgery for cancer.

Our boys were nine, seven, and six. "Please, God," I bargained, "if Jim's cancer doesn't return, I swear I will teach Sunday school for the rest of my life!"

A year later, Jim's cancer returned—an inoperable tumor. I quit teaching Sunday school. Jim's prognosis was not good, but I didn't believe God would ever let me raise our three boys alone. I returned to college to complete my teaching certificate "just in case."

Jim died the day after I completed my student teaching. We buried him the morning of Christmas Eve, with the funeral procession passing through snowy streets crowded with last-minute shoppers. Nothing seemed real. I felt separated from the real world, and my feelings felt as frozen as the drifts of snow.

WHEN PEOPLE EXPERIENCE A SIGNIFICANT LOSS, a natural healing process begins. This is grief. Elisabeth Kübler-Ross described grief as occurring in stages. Others have described the process as emotional tasks to experience and complete. Both views, however, include a disorderly but predictable pattern of experience and movement toward healing.

Whether you see your grief process as occurring in stages or as composed of tasks, allow yourself to experience and express your grief. In doing so, you release energy, decrease emotional intensity, and shorten the duration of your grief work.

## SHOCK AND DENIAL

The first response to loss is often a numbness caused by shock and denial. It is the mind and body's way of protecting us from physical and emotional overload. The death may be accepted intellectually, but it is difficult to comprehend the reality emotionally. Shock and denial allow us to shut off the emotional part of ourselves until we are ready to grieve the loss. As we experience shock and denial, we may find ourselves doing what needs to be done with nearly robotic thought and action.

Grief cannot be resolved until we allow ourselves to release shock and denial. If prolonged, they rob us of life and healing. Grief can be postponed, but it cannot be avoided. It is impossible to repress painful feelings without also repressing love, joy, and peace. Suppressing and avoiding grief increases stress and depletes the body's energy. It can cause illness and keep us from participating fully in our relationships.

Human beings tend to hold on to denial. We fear change, we fear the unknown, we want to remain in control. Denial may run particularly strong among those who were raised to be stoic, who did not view the body, or who did not have an opportunity to say goodbye. Do your best to let go of denial and experience your grief. For some people, this means repeating details of the death or talking frequently about the deceased.

*I was on automatic. Going for the paper. Going
to bed. Taking out the garbage. One foot in front,
etc. Now chatting as if nothing had happened,
next crying in the shower.*

*My reputation for rational moves, out the window.
Kübler-Ross had words for this mess. A lot of good it
did me. I, who many times warned the bereaved not
to make any big decisions, sold your car in two days*

*unnecessarily. Now you are truly gone, and I sit here in
darkness, conjuring a new meaning of place,
where form and substance are insignificant,
and time shall be no more.*

— Rev. Charles Brackbill

From *The Cancer Poetry Project,* edited by Karin B. Miller; adapted with permission.

## DESPAIR AND DISORGANIZATION

Understandably, the bereaved are often afraid of the powerful feelings accompanying grief, thinking they will shatter, be overwhelmed, go crazy, or fall into an inescapable pit of despair. This is normal. The many feelings of grief are powerful and frightening. As you slowly let go of your denial and experience these feelings, you will heal and gain a sense of confidence, trust, and integration.

While grieving, it is natural to experience a full range of emotions, and it is possible to recognize and accept them while learning appropriate ways to express them. You will even experience contradictory feelings. This is called ambivalence, and it can cause stress and anxiety, a sense of mild nervousness to frightening panic attacks. Ambivalence is your mind's way of attempting to both protest and accept your loss at the same time.

You may catch yourself using defenses—masks or behaviors—to hide painful emotions from yourself or others. Common defenses include joking, clowning, daydreaming, blaming, pleasing, sarcasm, silence, lying, and constant talking. While defenses can bring some measure of comfort, they can also obstruct the grief process, preventing you from feeling and releasing despair. Therefore, it's important to be aware of your defenses and strive to keep them to a minimum.

As you learn to identify, experience, and release your true feelings, you will come to feel more healthy and whole. Multiple losses or unresolved grief from the past may complicate this process and increase your sense of fear, disorganization, and your use of defenses. If you feel that you are unable to get at and experience your emotions, you may benefit from the help of a trained grief professional.

## REORGANIZATION AND ACCOMMODATION

Facing the pain of loss will bring healing, moving you toward acceptance, reorganization of self, and a greater understanding of the cycle of life. You will never be the same, but you will develop a new and rewarding connection with your deceased loved one as you memorialize his or her life and the time you shared. You will always have the love and memories he or she gave to you.

As you allow yourself to grieve to completion and learn the difficult lessons of letting go, you promote personal growth. You will become a more caring and compassionate person. At first you may fear losing other loved ones and either hold on too tightly or pull away to avoid more pain. In time, however, you will be able to let go and love freely again, and you will have a strengthened and healthy foundation for all your relationships.

# THE WORK OF GRIEVING

**PHASE I**   **SHOCK AND DENIAL**

Understand the cause of death.

Acknowledge the reality of the death.

Help plan and attend a funeral ritual.

Locate and accept support for your needs.

**PHASE II**   **DESPAIR AND DISORGANIZATION**

Gain courage to feel the pain of grief.

React to the separation and loss.

Read information about the dynamics of grief.

Recognize and express the many feelings of grief.

Take care of yourself physically.

Develop confidence in your ability to survive.

**PHASE III**   **REORGANIZATION AND ACCOMMODATION**

Review and make needed changes to old expectations and needs.

Choose appropriate ways to preserve the memory of your loved one.

Use the love and influence you received to live a meaningful life.

Develop a reason for being and a renewed sense of purpose.

Reinvest energy into satisfying skills, talents, and interests.

Nurture old relationships and develop new ones.

Celebrate your greater appreciation for life and relationships.

## GRIEF WORK EXERCISES

1) List other losses in your life and the ages at which you experienced them. Underline those that are still painful to think about.

2) Identify and record anything you may have done or may be doing as an attempt to deny the reality of your loved one's death. Are there times the death still seems unreal?

3) Determine which phase or phases of grief you are in now. Identify anything that might complicate your grief process or make it more difficult for you.

## JOURNAL

1) Write about your first responses to your loss. Include what you felt and did. Recall if you received support and comfort.

2) What has been most helpful in allowing you to accept the reality of your loss? What has been most painful?

3) Write a poem or draw a picture titled "Grief."

# REDUCING FEAR

B efore Jim died I was a very fearful person. I was afraid of frogs,
storms, winter driving. . . . My fears were often silly but powerful.
I was perhaps a little neurotic, very dependent, and not at all assertive.
I was, perhaps, afraid I could never survive without Jim. The week before
he died, some amazing grace swept away all my fears except one. I was
terribly afraid of the pain of grief.

As high school sweethearts we waited six years to be married, but we
were seldom in the same city for longer than two weeks. I longed for the
time we would not have to say goodbye, but, after our wedding, Jim's job
involved traveling. I always remembered the terrible physical pain I felt in
my heart when he left on his first trip . . . and it was only a three-day trip.

When he died, I feared the pain of that permanent separation.
I truly thought it would be so great it would kill me. I repressed my
grief for a long time.

I avoided driving near the hospital where Jim died, but several
months later my son was injured in a hockey game. His nose was badly
cut and a doctor in the crowd suggested I take him to the emergency
room for X-rays. Fear must have crowded my face, because he asked if
I was all right. "I can't go there," I hesitated. "My husband just died
there!" I did go, however, and again a few days later to take him in for
surgery on his broken nose. It was difficult for both of us. He needed his
father . . . and I did, too.

FEAR IS A NATURAL REACTION to a real or imagined threat to physical or emotional security. When fearful, our reaction is either to run away or stay and fight. Most fears develop from early conditioning and experiences. Situations of powerlessness increase fear. Fear of death is perhaps the most basic of our fears.

## DEATH AND FEAR

Our ultimate powerlessness over death and the loss of those we love is frightening. The painful feelings and uncertainty of death also make fear a natural emotion of the grief experience.

Many people try to distract or avoid or deny their fears about death. They worry about death or try to prevent death from happening. Some people build emotional walls, not allowing themselves to get close to others or to love fully. Others attempt to deny their fears. All of these behaviors can cause physical problems such as nausea, headaches, and insomnia, as well as psychological problems such as anxiety, depression, and obsessive-compulsiveness. As with the other emotions of grief, we heal by facing and feeling our fear.

Some people believe that they sense the presence of the deceased. They may fear they are going crazy, especially if they experience visual, tactile, or auditory signs. While frightening, these experiences are actually quite common and can promote a sense of faith and security when shared. Although such experiences seem to be real, many professionals doubt the reality and see them as an attempt to deny the loss.

## COPING WITH FEAR

Coping with fear begins with awareness. When we are aware of our fears, we can learn either to live with them or to release them. Facing and addressing fear is empowering. It helps us learn to risk failure, as well as to distinguish what we can and cannot control.

Coping with fear is a personal experience, though several strategies work well for many people. Think about your fears surrounding the loss of your loved one. Allow them to surface and come to consciousness. Write out your fears in your journal. Determine what you need to feel safe (soothing music, prayer, meditation, and humor help) and take small steps to conquer your fears.

Share your fears with your higher power, a trusted friend, and your support network. Ask your higher power for help in feeling and releasing your fears. Expressing your fears to others will free you of the burden of carrying them alone, helping you gain perspective and increase your sense of safety.

## GRIEF WORK EXERCISES

1) To increase your awareness of where your feelings are located and how you express them, do the exercise on page 30. Determine if you get aches and pains in the same places you repress fear or anger.

2) Make a list of your fears. Be specific. What is your most painful fear? What is your most humorous fear? Place a star by the fears you can do something about. Then, share one or more of your fears with someone you trust.

3) List small steps you can take to conquer your fears. Imagine yourself conquering your fear.

## JOURNAL

1) Your feelings may surface in your dreams. Describe any disturbing dreams you have had. Then, describe any comforting dreams you have had.

2) Do you (or anyone else you know) believe that you have sensed the presence of the deceased? Describe when, where, and what it felt like.

3) List places or things that are difficult reminders of your loss. Write out what you could do to cope with these difficult situations, places, and fears. What would help you feel safe? Begin to confront uncomfortable situations one at a time as you are able.

# FEELING PERSON EXERCISE

FEELINGS ARE SOMETHING YOU FEEL SOMEPLACE IN YOUR BODY. Close your eyes and think about a time when you felt really angry. Determine where in your body you feel anger. Scribble that area or areas with a red crayon. Do the same thing for your other feelings, using different colors for each feeling.

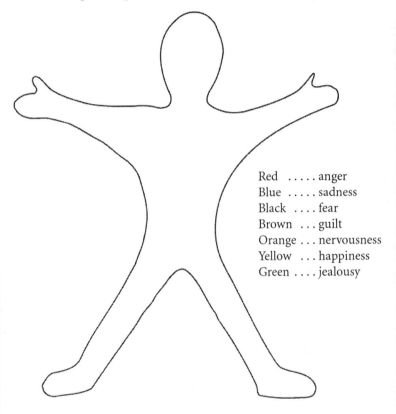

Red ..... anger
Blue ..... sadness
Black .... fear
Brown ... guilt
Orange ... nervousness
Yellow ... happiness
Green .... jealousy

Feelings that are repressed often cause physical problems. Do you get aches and pains in the same places where you store anger, fear, or other feelings?

From *When Someone Very Special Dies* by Marge Eaton Heegaard, adapted with permission.

# Expressing Anger
# in Healthy Ways

I was angry at the doctor who gave Jim a prescription for a tranquilizer instead of discovering the cancer.

I was angry at his family for leaving most of an estate, in English tradition, to the oldest son and causing distress to Jim, the second son.

I was even angry one day at Jim for "spoiling" our sons and then abandoning me to raise them alone.

But I was a good Scandinavian girl. I had a difficult time recognizing, and even more trouble expressing, anger. I was better at rationalizing and intellectualizing. My feelings were all in my head.

My sister and I took turns helping Mother take care of Dad at home. He was near death, but it was time for my sister to leave and return to New Mexico. She was the oldest, and usually the wisest, and was giving me lots of advice. I had done some work with hospice and had ideas of my own, but I was also angry at God for letting death be so difficult. "You don't know anything about this!" I shouted at her. "You think you know everything, but you don't!"

Somehow she knew I wasn't angry at her. I was afraid to be left alone for his death, and I was angry at the situation. Instead of getting defensive, she put her arms around me and said, "It will be okay. We can't fight now."

Dad died the next day and my brother and his family were with us.

ANGER IS AN EMOTIONAL RESPONSE to frustration and perceived injustice. Something is taken away or wishes are not being fulfilled. Frustration, fear, abandonment, and hurt often lie below anger. The root of anger is often something that makes a person feel small and helpless, so it is not surprising that most people feel anger when a loved one dies.

So many of us, however, believe that it is not okay to feel this anger and express it. Anger is acceptable and normal. If we don't feel and express it in healthy ways, our anger will come out in behavior that is not healthy or acceptable.

## MASKING ANGER

We learn to repress anger early on. Children naturally feel anger in their hands, feet, or mouths and want to hit, kick, or scream when angry. When they learn this is not acceptable but do not learn healthy ways to express their anger, they repress it. Their anger moves into other parts of their bodies, causing physical problems such as headaches or stomachaches. It eventually escapes as rage or hardens into resentment.

If we do not learn healthy ways to express our anger, we continue to deny and repress it as adults. We soften the truth of our anger, for example, with words such as annoyed, disgusted, irritated, and hurt. We mask our anger. Sarcasm, gossiping, martyrdom, chronic forgetfulness, tardiness, depression, and clumsiness are some of the emotional and behavioral masks of anger.

While historically it has been more acceptable for men to express anger than women, both men and women mask their anger. Men may, for example, become sullen, withdrawn, or stoic. Women may turn anger into sadness or fear. It's not surprising, then, that many adults have a hard time recognizing, feeling, expressing, and accepting their anger. As with children, this anger can escape as rage or harden into resentment.

# EXPERIENCING, EXPRESSING, AND RELEASING ANGER

It is natural to feel cheated and abandoned when a loved one dies. The death is a great loss and a seeming injustice. It is normal to feel angry at anyone or anything that contributed to the death. It is also normal to feel anger at the one who died and left you. But if you do not feel, express, and release your anger, it will be misdirected at friends, family members, medical personnel, funeral directors, spiritual leaders, and your higher power.

When expressing and releasing anger, it is important to consider the consequences of your actions. Anger does not have to be reasonable or sensible, but it carries the risk of triggering defensive reactions in others.

Simple anger usually lasts just a few seconds, but unexpressed anger can lead to resentment. When individuals make you angry, sometimes you need to confront them and let them know how you feel. Other times you may decide not to let their crazy behavior destroy your inner peace, choosing instead to let go of your resentment.

ACCEPTANCE

*Acceptance is the answer.*
*The serenity comes then.*
*It comes flowing in*
  *and envelops you in its arms.*
*It is a peace*
  *that passes all understanding.*

— Elise L. Hesser

## GRIEF WORK EXERCISES

1) Make a list of instances in which you have felt angry. Check (√) those you have expressed in healthy ways. Star (*) those you still feel resentful about. Determine ways you can resolve your resentment.

2) How do you react when feeling angry? Which suggestions in the Expressing Anger list (see page 36) would seem most effective for you?

3) Draw a simple symbol to represent someone or something you feel anger toward. Using a red crayon, scribble it out until you feel your anger is released.

## JOURNAL

1) Write about any anger you do not feel comfortable sharing with others.

2) Identify any anger you may have misdirected. How might you express that anger to the appropriate person in a healthy way? Decide how you should make amends if your misdirected anger hurt someone.

3) Express angry feelings in a letter you don't intend to send. Tear the letter in small pieces and throw it away.

# EXPRESSING ANGER

EVERYONE GETS ANGRY at the loss of a loved one. Everyone. It is okay to feel anger toward the person who died; the person, illness, or situation that caused the death; and anything or anyone contributing to the death. It is not okay to hate yourself; threaten to harm yourself or others; or harm yourself, others, or things.

## ACCEPTABLE WAYS TO EXPRESS ANGER

- Pause for a count of ten.
- Talk about it directly.
- Write it out, then tear up the angry thoughts or scribble them out with a red crayon.
- Exercise or play sports.
- Stomp (privately) or run.
- Engage in a throwing motion (i.e., play catch).
- Play an instrument.
- Yell in the shower or other private place.
- Punch a bag or pillow.

## TECHNIQUES FOR SHARING YOUR ANGER WITH OTHERS

1) Decide what you are really angry about.
2) Release some anger in one of the ways suggested above.
3) Share your feelings with the person you are angry at (if possible and appropriate) or with a trusted other. Use "I" messages ("you" messages provoke defensiveness):

    I am angry because. . . .
    I feel. . . .
    I need/want. . . .

4) Listen carefully to the response and try to understand.
5) Make an appropriate response that does not escalate the situation.

# Resolving Guilt

Jim wanted me to marry again if he should die. I raised the boys alone for six years because I didn't want to risk further loss and pain by loving again. I felt guilty. I once asked my youngest son if he resented the fact that I had not found another daddy for him. He didn't. I was carrying guilt I didn't need to feel.

I do have some regrets. Jim and I didn't talk about his dying. We talked about the "IF" and made necessary plans, but we seldom shared our feelings. We denied the negatives we were being told and protected each other from our worries. We missed the opportunity for sharing one of life's most intimate and important times. I think, now, how lonely it must have been for him to be unable to share his fears with me.

I also regret the way I tried to deny the reality of his death. I insisted on a closed casket. It was popular at the time, but I know now it was a mistake. Children weren't allowed hospital visiting privileges, and the boys were not prepared for their father's death. I was unable to model healthy grieving.

I came to my work with grief and loss from my own mistakes, sharing what I have learned from experience as well as education. I cannot go back and live my own life differently, but I am happy knowing my work and my books have made a difference in the lives of others.

GUILT IS A UNIQUELY HUMAN EMOTION. Our guilt can be real or assumed. The challenge, especially with the loss of a loved one, is to distinguish real guilt from assumed guilt. In doing so we learn what we are responsible for and what we are not responsible for, freeing ourselves to move toward acceptance of self, others, and the way things are.

## REAL GUILT AND ASSUMED GUILT

Real guilt comes from doing something truly hurtful to another person. It is a healthy emotion because it develops and maintains our conscience and teaches compassion. Real guilt holds us accountable for our behavior and is correctable. It can be dealt with in the following way:

1) Ask yourself:
   - What did I do to really hurt someone else or myself?
   - Was it intentional?
   - Could it have been avoided?
   - If so, how?
2) Confess and apologize.
3) Find some way to make amends.
4) Receive forgiveness.
5) Change guilt-producing behavior if possible.

Assumed guilt happens when we allow ourselves to become victims of external pressures, exaggerated ideals, and perfectionism. It is unhealthy because it demands that we assume responsibility out of proportion to our real involvement. It is destructive because it is shame-based, telling us that who we are is not okay and that there is nothing we can do about it.

Patterns of assumed guilt often begin when we are children, especially if we grew up accused of being bad or deficient because of our behavior. The result of this assumed guilt is that we grow up convinced that we are responsible for things out of our control and that we are bad and need to be punished.

## SURVIVOR GUILT

When a loved one dies, most people feel some guilt about what they did or did not do, said or did not say. This is survivor guilt. We may feel guilty about grieving too much or too little. Some of us feel we failed to live up to certain standards. We also may feel guilty simply because we are still alive. Much survivor guilt is assumed.

Society encourages such high and unrealistic standards that we are all at risk for survivor guilt. Most people, for example, wish they had been more available, had never been angry, had shown more love before their loved one died. But realistically, no one can be 100 percent available; our lives are full of necessary commitments that distract us and demand our time. Anger, too, is normal and inevitable, even in the best relationships. We often speak harshly to those we love the most. No one can remain constantly patient and even-tempered with those they love.

Sometimes, we assume guilt or hold on to our guilt as an attempt to deny our lack of control over death. It is normal to do so, but hanging on to this guilt is self-destructive. It prevents us from moving toward acceptance, produces fear and anxiety, triggers mental suffering and emotionally-induced illness, and impairs our relationships.

## SHARING AND HEALING GUILT

Feelings of guilt need to be shared with others who can help you determine whether your guilt is real or assumed. "Oughts" and "shoulds" need to be examined and, if deemed unrealistic and destructive, discarded.

Hearing family, friends, or members of a grief support group share unreasonable feelings of responsibility for causing or not preventing a death will often help you recognize your own unrealistic expectations. It is important to learn to recognize excessive and inappropriate guilt and release it.

Forgiveness and change heal real guilt. Forgive others for what they did out of ignorance, fear, or pain. Forgive yourself for similar and other imperfections. Seek forgiveness from your deceased loved one and your higher power. Trust that you are forgiven. Accept the forgiveness you receive. It can bring a remarkable sense of release. Complete your healing by striving to change your guilt-producing behaviors. If you are unable to resolve your guilt, seek the help of a grief counselor.

# WILL I ALWAYS FEEL GUILTY?

GUILT WHISPERS THROUGH US. It grows until we feel an agony of remorse and regret. There are those things we wish we hadn't done, and unkind words we wish we hadn't spoken. Just as troublesome as what we did and said are the things we didn't do, the words we didn't say.

Too often in the past we let our loving feelings go unexpressed. We should have touched more gently and spoken with greater concern. We could have listened with our full attention and loved more completely, but the days were busy and we were preoccupied with our own lives. It was so easy to let time slip away because we believed there was always going to be another tomorrow for us.

Now that it is tomorrow—and too late—we rail at ourselves. Guilt saps us of energy. We toss about as we seek the peace of sleep. Questions of "Why did I. . . ?" and "Why didn't I. . . ?" come as if they will never end. But end they will. Among the insightful writings of the poet Elle Wheeler Wilcox is the assurance that we will eventually find peace with ourselves:

> *This, too, will pass away: absorb the thought,*
> *And wait—your waiting will not be in vain,*
> *The dark today leads into light tomorrow:*
> *There is not endless joy, no endless sorrow.*

As time diminishes our grief, the hurtful past will fade. Our inner whisperings about "What should have been" or "What might have been" will grow ever more faint. In their place will be fond memories to cherish.

From *Beyond Sorrow* by Herb and Mary Montgomery; printed with permission.

## GRIEF WORK EXERCISES

1)   Finish the statement, "If only I did not. . . ."

2)   Finish the statement, "If only I had. . . ."

3) Share your feelings of guilt with someone you trust to help you gain greater perspective. List who you can talk to and why.

## JOURNAL

1) Create a guilt inventory, listing reasons the death was or wasn't your fault, then list any regrets you have concerning the things you did or did not do or say before your loved one died. Write about why each might be a case of real or assumed guilt. Avoid using the words *should* or *ought.*

2) Decide what you can do about real guilt. Write about how you can make amends.

3) Write a letter to your loved one. Thank him or her for enriching your life. Express your "if onlys" and other regrets. Say goodbye and ask to be released. Imagine his or her response.

# Managing Depression

I nterested in my family's medical history, I asked my father about his brother who died from a heart attack at an early age. Mother called me into the kitchen where she told me to stop asking questions. "Your uncle committed suicide," she told me. "He became an alcoholic after his wife died and suffered financial problems. . . . Your father still can't talk about it."

Jean was perhaps the most creative and intelligent person I ever knew. Her home was furnished with beautiful antiques she had refinished herself, an enormous rug she had braided, lovely pictures she had painted and framed. She served home-canned peaches after delicious dinner parties.

She was a witty friend and a loving wife and mother, but she killed herself because she thought her family would be better off without her. "She couldn't see herself as we did," the minister said at her funeral. She couldn't see reality because she had clinical depression.

My life was difficult and painful at times, and I even envied Jim his death. I thought of suicide, and it scared me. I didn't know anything about depression or suicide, and I didn't want to do anything that would cause my children more pain. I was fortunate that I was not clinically depressed. I could see reality, and I knew that suicide was no answer to temporary problems.

GRIEF, LIKE A NUMBER OF OTHER PAINFUL EXPERIENCES, will produce some feelings that are difficult and uncomfortable, but they are usually temporary. Feelings of uncertainty, helplessness, and despair are common.

For most of our lives, we have some control over circumstances, but when death occurs, we are forced to confront our powerlessness. Our self-esteem sinks. We cannot go back and change anything, and we feel completely helpless, like a child. We often react to our feelings and sense of helplessness by becoming depressed.

## THE DEPRESSIVE RESPONSE

When the difficult feelings of grief are not processed, they can be turned inward, producing depression. Symptoms of depression include sluggishness, fatigue, restlessness, anxiety, and loss of interest in life. It is common for a bereaved person to feel hypersensitive to criticism or become sharp and irritable with those most concerned with his or her welfare—and then become more depressed by such reactions. People who are depressed are often their most severe critics. With painful self-judgment, they often feel unworthy of the love of others.

People sometimes try to escape depression through trivial pastimes or frenetic activity, but self-esteem seems to increase only by making peace within. This may seem almost impossible to do. It does take time, but most bereaved persons resolve their depression and emerge healthy and well-organized. Those unable to do so may need counseling and medical help.

## CLINICAL AND REACTIVE DEPRESSION

Depression can be divided into two basic types: clinical depression and reactive depression. Clinical depression is less common and more serious than reactive depression. It is caused by a chemical imbalance in the brain and can occur without clear cause.

The death of a loved one can complicate clinical depression. If you have a personal or family history of clinical depression (or your depression goes unabated for more than four weeks) seek the help of a mental health professional. Clinical depression can be managed with medications, allowing you to work through your reactive depression.

Reactive depression is an emotional reaction after an event. It produces symptoms similar to clinical depression, but, drawing on one's own or other resources, the depressed person can usually restore balance in time.

The death of a loved one will almost always cause reactive depression. For example, the bereaved often feel that life has lost its meaning: Nothing seems to matter anymore. Simple tasks become difficult. All efforts seem useless. Those who are grieving frequently feel abandoned by God or a higher power. These painful times, however, often lead to spiritual and personal growth.

The bereaved often feel worthless because they were unable to prevent the death. Sometimes they feel irritable and hostile toward their loved one for dying and leaving them all alone. Widowed parents are overwhelmed with new responsibilities. If the loved one died after a long illness, caretakers may be exhausted and unable to think clearly enough to make important decisions. It is important for the bereaved to evaluate what can and cannot be controlled, redefining their goals and expectations.

Mourning is a badge of loving that can be worn proudly. All love eventually leads to suffering, and suffering deepens humanity. It is hard, but it's important not to fear loving again. It is also vital to know that joy and sadness are independent emotions that can mix well together. This is evident at both weddings and funerals. It is all right to find humor in the midst of sadness. Both tears and laughter are healing.

## GRIEF WORK EXERCISES

1) List the times and places where you feel comfortable crying.

2) Make a list of chores and other activities that you are expected to do this week. Cross out those that can wait. Draw a smile after those that someone else can do for you. Draw a star on something you will do tomorrow.

3) Have you ever been treated for depression? If so, list the symptoms you experienced at that time. This loss may require you to begin medication again. See your physician or psychiatrist.

## JOURNAL

1) Make a list of what you have accomplished this week. What was most difficult? What made it difficult? Congratulate yourself.

2) List the anger and fears that you have not expressed. Write about how these might be adding to your depression.

3) Name the people who need you. Acknowledge the pain and suffering your death would cause them, then write how you can take better care of yourself.

# COPING WITH DEPRESSION

- A significant loss will always trigger some depression.

- Emotional ups and downs are a normal part of the grief process. Anticipate the lows and plan how you will get through them. Remember, it won't last forever.

- Identify the expectations and responsibilities that most trouble you. Make a list of what you have to do each day.

- Anger turned inward is often the root of depression. Express your anger in acceptable ways.

- Keep interested in other people and their lives. Caring about others helps you keep problems in perspective.

- Avoid depressive situations and people who minimize your feelings or suggest dreadful consequences.

- Plan ahead for holidays, anniversaries, and special days. Try to be with supportive people to share memories and feelings.

- Apologize if you have been antagonistic or have offended someone. Bereaved people are easily irritated when depressed.

- Develop a regular exercise plan to relieve tension. A daily walk, especially with a good friend, will be helpful. You can always work up to other exercises if you choose.

- Examine your feelings of helplessness and your need to control life events. Are you carrying feelings of responsibility and guilt rather than admitting helplessness?

- Goals and expectations may need to be redefined. Accept your best efforts rather than seek perfection.

- It is not unusual for the bereaved to have thoughts of suicide to end their pain or to join the deceased. These thoughts are serious and dangerous if they continue. If you are experiencing persistent thoughts of suicide, contact a mental health professional, your local suicide prevention center, a crisis center, or an emergency room immediately. Or, call 1-800-SUICIDE (1-800-784-2437).

# Identifying Childhood
# Losses and Family Issues

Dickie was our family's dog, but I considered him mine because we grew up together. He disappeared when I was twelve, and I remember not asking about him because I didn't want to be told he was dead. No one did. We didn't grieve, and we didn't get another pet. No one wanted to risk another loss . . . so we missed out on the joys of living and loving.

Our family didn't deal well with loss. My grandparents from both sides emigrated from Sweden, leaving behind everyone and everything. Denial may have been the only way they could cope. My mother's parents both died when she was an infant, and her foster father died when she was seven. I learned my pattern of denial from my family at an early age.

Tom was identified as the cat that bit a small child in a neighborhood several blocks away. We thought Tom was a wonderful cat and would never do such a thing, but we kept him inside for the rabies observation period. When he was able to go out again, he immediately returned to that same area and bit my son, who went to retrieve him.

"We can't keep Tom," I told the boys. "We can't risk that happening again." There were protests, but my decision was made. I took Tom to the Humane Society while the boys were in school. Crying and unable to talk, I filled in some forms and left without Tom.

"Are they going to kill him?" Jim asked when he returned from school. I told him I hadn't asked. "Then he'll spend the rest of his life *trying to find us!" he shouted angrily at me, adding a few swear words, which was very unlike him.*

*Jon came home next and asked about Tom. "Then you'll have to buy us a dog," he threatened, trying to replace his loss.*

*Michael came home last, and when he learned about Tom, he went up to his room and sobbed loudly for a long time. A time of silence followed before he called me to his room. It looked as if half of his belongings had been moved into the hall. "Please do something with these things. They all remind me of you, and I can't bare to think of you anymore."*

*Each of the boys had responded differently to their loss. It had been less than a year since their father had died. I knew I hadn't handled this very well. "I loved that cat, too," I cried, and we finally cried together.*

CHILDREN GRIEVE DIFFERENTLY THAN ADULTS. They are emotionally unable to sustain feelings of grief, and they often wait to make sure other loved ones are okay before they grieve. So, when someone special dies, they may appear unaffected by the loss. Children repress their feelings. They may try to give comfort (instead of seek it) to protect grieving parents. They often cry alone in their rooms to hide feelings that they believe are babyish. Most adults go unaware of the painful grief a child feels, so the child does not receive needed comfort and support.

As a result, children often grow up with unresolved grief or unhealthy coping patterns, which can hinder or complicate the adult grieving process. It is helpful to look back on your early losses with the maturity and understanding of an adult, to grieve these losses, and to identify unhealthy grieving patterns. Once you recognize these patterns, you can change them. In so doing, you will mirror healthy patterns of grieving to other family members.

# EARLY LOSS RECALL

The following is a guided meditation to help you identify your reactions to early losses. Find a time and place where you can relax without interruption for about twenty minutes. Have paper and a small box of crayons available. You will want to draw a picture of what you recall, because it will help you remember more details. Drawing also gives you a sense of control over a time when you probably felt helpless. Use the following suggestions to guide your meditation.

*Close your eyes and imagine yourself as the small child you once were. Try to remember how you looked, what was important to you, and what you did.*

*Think about an elementary school you attended when you were about eight or nine years old. Remember what you can about the classroom: windows, blackboards, locker or place for jackets, teacher's desk, your desk, and so on. Imagine being there again and recall what you can about the child you were. Did you have many friends or were you a lonely child? Did you like your teacher and did your teacher like you? Did you like or dislike school? What did you like least and most about school?*

*Next, imagine the school day ends and you return home. Imagine yourself going by bus, bike, foot, or any way you would have gone. Recall what you can about the neighborhood, your yard, and the exterior of your house.*

*Imagine going inside, using a door you would have used. Walk around inside, remembering what you can about the different rooms. Choose a room where you felt safe or most comfortable, and think about what you liked about that room.*

*Again, think about the child you once were and what was important to you then. Remember losing something or someone important to you. It could be a toy, a pet, a person . . . anything, even a place you lived prior to a move.*

*A picture about this event has probably been forming in your mind. Think about the picture for a moment. Then, open your eyes. Using* crayons, begin to draw the picture. Don't worry about your drawing ability. You're just trying to remember more about the event so you can learn about yourself and how you coped with loss and change.

When you finish drawing, write a few words on the back of the paper. Briefly describe:

- how you felt,
- what you did,
- what others did, and
- whether you were comforted by someone.

Finally, close your eyes and imagine yourself being comforted over the loss in a way you would have liked. Allow yourself as much time as you need before you open your eyes again and return to your adult world. Examine the descriptive words you wrote on the back of your drawing and look for any similarities to what you are thinking, feeling, and doing in relation to your current loss.

This exercise can be repeated for any stage in your life. It will help bring back many feelings of unresolved grief. Most adults do not remember being comforted when they were young because they didn't let anyone know how they were feeling. As an adult, you can now look back on that time with more understanding. You will gain insights into any unhealthy patterns you may have developed and allow yourself to let them go, replacing them with healthy methods of grieving.

# PATTERNS FOR COPING WITH LOSS

### DEFENSES

People who didn't receive support or comfort as a child are likely to develop defenses to protect themselves from pain. As adults, they may not expect comfort and may even reject it when it is offered. Sometimes defenses are necessary, but they can become habitual, evolving into walls or masks that keep people from feeling close to you. Common defenses include:

*Denial.* If you cannot remember any losses as a child or you were taught to repress your feelings, denial could be your pattern. Many cultures for many generations were taught to be stoic and to repress negative feelings. Those in denial may rationalize and make excuses for, or find other ways to avoid, painful feelings. They may intellectualize rather than feel their pain.

*Replacement.* A relationship needs to be grieved when it ends before a healthy new relationship can begin. Some people, however, will avoid feelings of grief by replacing a deceased loved one before their mourning is complete. For example, pets are easy to replace, particularly in rural areas, and many people will avoid their feelings of grief by getting a new pet soon after their old one dies. Widows and widowers, too, will sometimes remarry rather than mourn.

*Anger.* Anger is a natural part of grief, but inappropriate or misdirected anger is not healthy. Family conflicts often flair up during times of stress, and this can seriously impair relationships. Sadly, families often fight instead of cry together.

*Guilt.* Some guilt feelings early in the grief process are normal, but if you continue to feel responsible for causing or failing to prevent the death, this can indicate an unhealthy pattern. Children who experience a significant loss during their "magical thinking years" often develop a false sense of power over events; as adults, they may continue to feel overly responsible for anything that happens.

## CRYING

Crying is a healthy expression of sadness. If you remember crying and receiving comfort, you are fortunate. You may be a person who cries easily and perhaps feels embarrassed, but people will know how you feel. You are more likely to expect and receive comfort from others. Crying is only unhealthy if it is used to manipulate others to get your needs met.

There are times and places where crying may not seem appropriate, but it is important to find time to release sad feelings. Music often helps people cry after the death of a loved one. Children may be disturbed to see adults crying, but they can learn that crying helps let the sadness out.

## GRIEVING FAMILIES

A death in the immediate family brings stress and disruption to the family system. Grieving family members have a difficult time supporting each other because each person grieves the loss of a different personal relationship.

In some families, hurt and resentment flair up, leading to arguments and regrettable expressions of anger. When feelings are not shared, however, it can seem as if family members are not grieving at all.

The death of a spouse or partner completely changes the survivor's world. It brings a loss of identity, as well as a need to play new roles and develop new skills. Widowed parents feel overwhelmed at the thought of taking sole responsibility for the home and children. Furthermore, it is difficult to balance the need to mourn with the need to parent. Mourning is sometimes delayed until more energy and support are available.

Those widowed in their later years struggle with loneliness. They often feel excluded from couple-oriented events and find it difficult to travel alone. They face a difficult adjustment. They may need to become more independent, develop new interests, and learn to cope with new responsibilities. As they gain new skills, their confidence and self-esteem increase.

When a child dies, a strong bond is broken, creating a long and painful grief. The parents are challenged with old and new conflicts. If one partner seeks closeness while the other needs space to replenish his or her energy, grief turns inward, threatening communication and self-worth. Secondary losses are many, making the death of a child the most difficult to grieve.

Death changes the family dynamic for children, too, interrupting normal routines and damaging the children's sense of security. When a sibling dies, the surviving children often feel inferior to the special deceased child; they may try too hard to be perfect or to make their parents happy, or they may get in trouble to gain attention. When a parent dies, children may try to take on roles vacated by the deceased, adult roles for which they are unprepared. The death of a parent is very traumatic and can leave children with both psychological and behavioral problems if grief is not resolved.

## COPING WITH FAMILY ISSUES AND GRIEF

One person's death can change the entire family structure. Often, old roles will need to be redefined and new roles assumed. Some members will feel the loss more strongly than others, and family members may try to protect each other by hiding feelings rather than sharing them in healthy ways. Family members cannot rescue each other from the pain of grief. They need to talk together, share their feelings and their memories of the deceased, and make important decisions together.

Families should not expect children to fill the void of a deceased sibling or parent. If children take on responsibilities beyond their capabilities, it can rob them of their childhood. Support from extended family and friends is important to comfort survivors and provide children with both male and female role models.

The double task of mourning and reorganizing the family is a challenge that requires social and emotional support as well as education. There are many books available to help you cope with loss and grief. Also, most communities offer support groups in schools, hospitals, and places of worship, creating a nonthreatening atmosphere where participants can share and learn from each other. If such support is not available and you need additional help, find an individual or family counselor with training in grief counseling.

## Letting Go

*I cried real tears of grief*
 *the deepest grief one can imagine.*
*The grief of "letting go."*
 *It's the hardest kind.*
*Letting go of the past events*
 *of the future accomplishments*
 *of the dreams you had.*
*The task is a formidable one.*

*I cried many tears of grief*
 *yesterday and the day before.*
*And I'm sure there are many*
 *tears left for me to shed.*
*But someday I will finally*
 *"let go" of what was, and*
 *I will accept "what is."*
*The task is not an impossible one.*

    — Elise L. Hesser

# HOW ADULTS CAN HELP CHILDREN
# COPE WITH DEATH AND GRIEF

CHILDREN MAY FEEL FRIGHTENED AND INSECURE because they sense the grief and stress of others and feel powerless to help. They will need additional love, support, and structure in their daily routine.

When someone dies, children often worry about themselves and others dying. They need to know who would take care of them in the unlikely death of both parents.

They need an adequate explanation of the cause of death, using correct terms like "die" and "dead." Using vague terms and trying to shield them from the truth merely adds confusion. Avoid terms that associate going away, sleep, or sickness with death.

Children have magical thinking and may believe that their behavior or thoughts can cause or reverse death.

Do not exclude children when family or friends come to comfort grieving adults. Avoidance or silence teaches children that death is a taboo subject. Children need to learn how to cope with loss, not be protected from grief.

Help children to recognize, name, accept, and express feelings to avoid developing unhealthy defenses to cope with difficult emotions. Make physical and creative activities available for energy outlets.

A child may try to protect grieving adults and attempt to assume the caretaker role, but children need to grow up normally without being burdened with adult responsibilities.

Help children cope with other losses. The death of a pet is a significant loss for a child. The patterns for coping with loss and grief begin in early childhood and often continue through adulthood.

Share religious beliefs carefully. Children may fear or resent a higher power who takes to heaven someone they love and need.

Feelings of abandonment, helplessness, despair, anxiety, apathy, anger, guilt, and fear are common and often acted out aggressively because children may be unable to express feelings verbally.

From *When Someone Very Special Dies* by Marge Eaton Heegaard; adapted with permission.

## Grief Work Exercises

1) Do the guided meditation beginning on page 53 and draw your memories.

2) Write what you felt, what you did, and what others did at the time of your loss. Did you get comfort and support?

3) How did you cope with loss and change at that time (crying, denial, replacement, anger, guilt, and so forth)? Is your reaction to your current loss similar? Is it something you would like to change?

## JOURNAL

1) Write your thoughts about other losses from your childhood.

2) Recall how your parents and other relatives reacted to loss. Were their reactions similar to yours? Have your reactions changed? How so?

3) Write about how you are grieving as a family. How are others reacting to this loss? Are you sharing feelings and crying together, or are you becoming distant? Are children receiving death education and support, or have they been excluded?

# Spirituality

A boy came to our door selling playing cards when I was a child. "They are the instruments of the devil!" my maternal grandmother claimed and sent him away. My father was also raised in a strict church family, but as a child I attended a variety of church, vacation, and Sunday schools and found something worthwhile in each.

I was confirmed in the Lutheran Church but was a member of the Congregational Church for thirty-five years until recently returning to the Lutheran Church.

Church was, and is, very important to me. When Jim was sick I was certain he would beat the impossible odds and live. My faith didn't waiver when he died. I was certain God would protect me from harm and difficulty. It gave me a much-needed strength, but I also used my faith as an unhealthy crutch to avoid grief. When I finally accepted the fact that life is difficult and bad things happen, my childhood faith was challenged with doubts and questions, but I emerged from the struggle with a more sound and mature faith.

I was with both my father and Jim when they died. Jim, by then paraplegic, sat up moments before his death and waved away images unseen by me. At forty, he was still fighting death. My father, at eighty-eight, was ready. With both deaths, I felt it was a rare privilege to witness the passing of the spirit, confirming my belief in a spiritual afterlife.

DEATH REMINDS US OF HOW LITTLE CONTROL we have over life. Many people turn to their spirituality or faith when death seems unavoidable. Survivors of earthquakes and other disasters, for example, often credit a power greater than themselves with their survival.

When the opposite occurs and a loved one dies, the bereaved often feel abandoned by their higher power and wonder, "Why?" Others may argue that such tragedy is proof that there is no higher power guiding and protecting us, no beneficent order.

A great part of the grief process is a search for an answer to the why. Intellectually, we can learn *how* death occurs, but that doesn't always answer the emotional and spiritual question of *why*. Whether you are spiritual, religious, or uncertain in your beliefs, turning to a source greater than yourself and your understanding will guide you through your grief journey. It will help you find understanding and meaning in your loss.

## BLAME

Many of us have learned to define this higher power as all-powerful. We hold on to the image of a protector. We expect this higher power to keep us and everyone we love from harm—always. When someone we love dies, we feel betrayed and abandoned by the higher power. We often turn to blame.

Personal philosophies and religious faiths differ in their beliefs regarding whether a higher power causes or allows tragedy to end life. In Judaism, Islam, and Christianity, for example, the Old Testament offers many examples where God willfully punishes people. It is not unusual to wonder if our losses are punishment from a power greater than ourselves.

We may blame a higher power in an attempt to make sense of our loss and justify our anger. We gain comfort from this. If something can be blamed, it means that at least something is in control, something or someone can be held accountable. To believe this, we must envision an angry, vengeful power, one that is deceitful, fickle, exacting, and cold. As we blame, we create a belief system that explains our seeming loss, injustice, and abandonment, but such a perception lacks love and compassion.

## CHANGING PERSPECTIVE

Grief often changes our perspective of our higher power. Spiritual writings, both religious and secular, observe that free will seems to be at work in the universe. A higher power does not make things happen to reward or punish, does not spare one person and not another, but allows life to happen, free of orchestration. People, animals, and plants live and die as life plays out. And life includes tragedy, unfairness. Loved ones succumb to age and illness, die in accidents, fall victim to violence. They leave us too soon.

Yet love and compassion are present in this gift of free will. We are not alone in our independence. A higher power is there to help us understand and cope with life and loss. A protector is there to guide, comfort, and provide. A pattern of love and compassion emerges: there is some gift from every loss.

Whatever your faith or spirituality, strive to perceive a gentle and loving higher power at work in your grief and life. An example of this presence might be found in the mother bird. When she teaches her young to fly, she allows them to flail and flounder and to feel alone at times. But she is there, watching, ready to catch them before they fall too far. She does so because she knows they must learn to fly.

## MEND YOUR SPIRITUALITY

It is not unusual during the grief process to lose faith or feel angry at your higher power, or to turn away from your beliefs, spirituality, or faith. Express your anger and blame to your higher power. Unexpressed feelings prolong the pain and create a barrier between you and spiritual comfort at a time when you need it most.

Be open and honest with your higher power. Any good relationship has troubled times. It is all right to acknowledge and express anger at your higher power. It is human to question, to doubt, and to feel angry. It's how we find understanding. Risk trusting that your higher power will not abandon you. Many people find or develop hope, as well as faith and spirituality, when they share the entirety of their grief with a higher power.

Grief and loss test and strengthen our spirituality and faith, our belief in the unproven. Explore the presence, the loving work, of a higher power in your life—perhaps a deity, the universe, life, or nature. It's there. You will find the help, support, and guidance you need.

# GONE FROM MY SIGHT

I AM STANDING UPON THE SEASHORE. A ship at my side spreads her white sails to the morning breeze and starts for the blue ocean. She is an object of beauty and strength. I stand and watch her until at length she hangs like a speck of white cloud just where the sea and sky come to mingle with each other.

Then someone at my side says: "There, she is gone!"

"Gone where?"

Gone from my sight. That is all.

Her diminished size is in me, not in her. And just at the moment when someone at my side says: "There, she is gone!" there are other eyes watching her coming, and other voices ready to take up the glad shout: "Here she comes!"

And that is dying.

— Henry Van Dyke

## GRIEF WORK EXERCISES

1)  Finish the sentence, "Bad things happen to good people because. . . ."
    Evaluate this belief. Does it seem realistic? Healthy?

2)  Consider how your faith—or lack of faith—has affected your grief.
    How has grief affected your faith?

3) Write about the faith you had as a child. Has your faith changed as you have grown older? How so?

## JOURNAL

1) If you have a higher power, draw a picture or write a poem describing how this higher power is responding to you in your grief.

2) Express your anger to a higher power, to Death, to Nature, or to any other force you feel is operating in your life.

3) Write about the presence and comfort of a higher power in your life and the world around you. If you don't have a higher power, write about something that comforts you.

# COPING WITH STRESS

As the youngest child, I was taken care of by my entire family. After I grew up, I went from college to marriage to parenthood, remaining dependent on my husband. When our friends learned about Jim's condition, they wondered how I could cope alone. I didn't think I could.

Jim tried to protect me from pain. He didn't know it was only through pain that I would finally grow up and become a mature and confident adult.

Life was stressful after his death. There were injuries and illnesses. There were calls from my children's school decrying behavioral and learning problems. I didn't know then that children act out their feelings of grief. I found a policeman at my doorstep more than once. There was a house and yard to maintain, and financial and investment issues to consider. I gained help from my children, from wise and trusted friends, and from skilled professionals, but I also gained confidence in myself.

I prayed daily for wisdom, courage, and patience and thanked God for giving generously. I did things I would have considered impossible. I barely knew my way downtown when Jim died, but the second summer I drove the boys from Minnesota to New Mexico and back, visiting friends along the way. We found time to have fun.

Fortunately, I was able to stay in our home and avoid the change and stress that come with moving. I could avoid the stress of substitute teaching by doing freelance art work. It was also good therapy for me and provided contact with adults who had similar interests.

Perhaps most important . . . I didn't lose my sense of humor.

LOSS AND GRIEF ARE STRESSFUL. Understanding, recognizing, and managing your stress will help you lessen the discomfort of your grief experience.

## STRESS

There are varying degrees and different types of stress: mental, emotional, and physical. Not all stress is bad; stress can cause us to strive toward a goal or meet a deadline, increasing our confidence and self-esteem. However, unrelieved stress from intense or persistent anger, fear, and frustration can threaten health.

Aggressive emotions such as anger, impatience, worry, and fear cause the body to release hormones, including adrenaline, to prepare the body to survive a real or imagined danger. Prolonged release or repeated activation of this response stresses the mind and body and can lead to migraines, hypertension, heart disease, and stroke.

Passive emotions, such as despair, grief, and loneliness, register in another part of the brain and release other chemicals into the body. When this response is prolonged, it depresses the immune system, lowering the body's defenses against certain diseases, such as cancer, and precipitating other diseases, such as rheumatoid arthritis.

## SYMPTOMS OF STRESS

The death of a loved one is stressful. It challenges previous commitments, reminds us of our lack of control over life, and confuses our self-image. William Crisp, MD, director of the Stress Management Center in Phoenix, Arizona, identified the following symptoms of stress:

- insomnia and sleep interruption,
- inability to concentrate,
- loss of productivity and decision-making skills,
- decline in sexual responsiveness and ability to perform,

- frequent headaches, backaches, muscle spasms, or tiredness,
- frequent indigestion, diarrhea, or urination,
- cold hands,
- shortness of breath,
- frequent accidents and minor injuries,
- chronically hostile or angry feelings,
- frustration with minor annoyances, and
- neglect of self, in terms of leisure, rest, exercise, and diet.

You may recognize many of these symptoms as part of your grief experience. They are normal. Stress resulting from the death of a loved one cannot be avoided, but it can be minimized and managed.

## STRESS MANAGEMENT

Stress is part of being a living, feeling being. The death of a loved one, however, compounds a person's daily stress. Managing your stress during this difficult time is crucial for your physical and mental health. Your skills for coping with stress will develop as you practice them.

The ability to cope depends on a positive self-image and strong social support. Ruminating, withdrawing, and focusing on personal and situational regrets is stressful and can decrease one's ability to cope with loss.

Change must be anticipated and accepted because it is a natural part of life and growth. But change creates stress. Death, divorce, separation, marriage, a new job, the loss of a job, moving, and other personal changes are very stressful. Personal injury, illness, and legal or financial problems also create stress. After a death in the family, it is important to limit life changes as much as possible for two years. When this is not possible, recognize the fact that you must learn how to cope with the increased stress.

## Suggestions for Coping with Stress

*Develop* a positive mental picture of yourself, focusing on your strengths and abilities.

*Make time* for regular exercise. It is the best natural tranquilizer and sleeping pill. Find some exercise activity that you enjoy and will continue.

*Balance* work and play. Know your limits. Establish priorities and organize your time. Learn how to say no and become assertive.

*Plan* an adequate nutritional diet. It is normal to have an appetite change and to lose or gain weight while grieving. You will feel better if you eat regular meals that include all the food groups. Proteins, vegetables, fruits, and grains must be a part of your daily meals. Keep healthy snacks available.

*Recognize and accept* all feelings. Become aware of your losses and allow yourself to grieve them. Express your feelings. If you let others know how you really feel, they will be better prepared for their own eventual losses. Join a grief group where expression is encouraged.

*Share* worries and concerns with someone you trust, someone who will listen to you. Sharing with others will help you experience, feel, process, and release your pain.

*Journal* as a way to privately express and work through your feelings. A journal is a "good listener," never interrupting or talking back. Pain awakens creativity, so include poetry and drawings.

*Listen* to comforting and healing music. Doing so will help you relax and release your feelings. Listen to music you find motivational, too. It will give you strength and courage to do your grief work.

*Strive* to recognize what can and cannot be changed. Try to live one day at a time.

*Develop* your sense of humor. Humor can get you through the darkness. It is just as important to laugh as it is to cry.

*Listen* to relaxation tapes and practice relaxation techniques. Learn meditation, deep-breathing techniques, and visual imagery to rid your body of tension. You will feel calmer, more comfortable, and more capable of dealing with stress.

*Turn to* your faith or spirituality. You will feel less alone in your grief.

*Remember,* when the body is tired, exercise the mind. When the mind is tired, exercise the body.

FALLING APART

*I seem to be falling apart.*
*My attention span can be measured in seconds.*
*My patience in minutes.*
*I cry at the drop of a hat.*
*I forget things constantly.*
*The morning toast burns daily.*
*I forget to sign checks.*
*Half of everything in the house is misplaced.*
*Feelings of anxiety and restlessness are my constant companions.*
*Sunny days seem an outrage.*
*Other people's pain and frustrations seem insignificant.*
*Laughing, happy people seem out of place in my world.*
*It has become routine to feel half-crazy.*
*I am normal. I am told.*
*I am a newly grieving person.*

— Printed in a church newsletter many years ago

## Grief Work Exercises

1) Identify your stresses by listing the personal and family changes you have experienced in the past two years.

2) List what you can do to avoid more change and stress.

3) Evaluate your exercise and self-care program. List what you are doing and decide if you need to do more.

## JOURNAL

1) List the issues causing you the most concern and worry. Evaluate your list, then put an asterisk (*) next to those that should be addressed now. Create a plan for addressing the most pressing issues.

2) Write about something that makes you laugh. Laughter is healing. Identify the good things you still have in your life.

3) Make a list of ways you plan to reduce stress. Do one thing from your list today.

## ADDITIONAL STRESS FOLLOWING A LOSS

Put a check (√) next to any stressors you anticipate or have already experienced since your loved one's death.

_____ Confronting financial problems

_____ Talking with attorneys or medical personnel

_____ Settling the estate

_____ Informing acquaintances and business associates of the death

_____ Updating insurance policies, credit cards, and bank accounts

_____ Receiving survivor's benefits

_____ Anticipating holidays or family events

_____ Encountering problems with in-laws

_____ Helping children grieve

_____ Helping a spouse or partner grieve

_____ Battling family members for child custody

_____ Raising young children

_____ Watching older children leave home

_____ Suffering an illness or injury

_____ Losing or changing a job

_____ Traveling for business or pleasure

_____ Changing residence

_____ Adapting to new responsibilities

_____ Other:

_____ Other:

What can you do to make these less stressful?

# CHALLENGING LONELINESS AND FINDING SELF

J im did not leave me all alone. We had three sons, a cat with kittens, a rabbit, a variety of other pets boys collect if mothers are tolerant, and a house full of neighborhood children. I redecorated the house in cheerful colors, but we were still lonely. So we went to the Humane Society to find a dog that needed a home. She brightened our days.

It was 1969, and there was only one grief support group in the area, but I had no intention of going because I was certain there would be no one there under eighty. I should have. It was what I needed.

I had no family in town, but friends and neighbors were very supportive. I was not excluded from social events, but I often felt the most lonely in the midst of a large group discussing issues I could no longer relate to. My identity had changed, and I no longer knew who I was. Comfort came from opera music on a classical radio station, which woke me up and put me to sleep. It was nice to come home to if I went out, and it prevented the loneliness of silence while I was home.

I didn't want to meet single people because I didn't feel single. I definitely did not want to ever marry again and risk the pain of loss. I felt Jim's presence for a long time after his death, and I had a great deal of pride and some amazement at my ability to survive alone. Nevertheless, smiling enthusiasm masked my loneliness from my children, my friends, and even myself.

EDGAR JACKSON WROTE in *The Many Faces of Grief* that "loneliness accompanies grief as an assault on the meaning of life itself." It is a threat to a person's inner security system. When a loved one dies, you lose that part of yourself that was shared with another.

The loss often leaves a great empty space in your heart and life. (You could draw two circles showing how much your lives overlapped.) The emptiness is painful, generating questions of identity and feelings of loneliness. Your sense of identity will return as you take your grief journey, and your loneliness will begin to fade as you become strong enough to reopen your heart and share yourself with others.

## THE GRIEF JOURNEY IS
## A JOURNEY OF SELF-DISCOVERY

The loss of a relationship changes a person's sense of identity. With the death of a loved one, survivors often wonder, "Who am I now?" It is easy to confuse our identity with our relationships and our roles in them (lover, father, mother, child, friend). The loss of loved ones denies us these roles.

Grief forces us to know ourselves. It is partly an inward journey taken alone. It is lonely, but it is an important time for exploring and developing who we are, for discovering our true self. Strive to know your needs and wants, your likes and dislikes. Value your aloneness and grow comfortable with yourself. As you do, your identity will become known to you.

## ALLOW YOUR HEART TO HEAL AND OPEN

After the death of a loved one, there is a natural tendency to pull away from others and shut down for a time. It is true that the pain of loneliness can be so great that a person feels as if something inside has died. There is comfort in isolation. It is normal to want to avoid the pain of further loss by trying to disconnect from others and deny the process of love. It is normal to want to cocoon in order to reflect and gather strength.

But do not cocoon for too long. Do not allow your heart to harden. This can be truly tragic because it robs you of life and the world of your presence. Life becomes what it is through social relationships. With time and healing, you will learn to value your need for time alone *and* time with others.

The task is to begin again, to risk expressing and sharing your human capacity for love and care. Begin with your family and friends who comfort you. Accept their love and be willing to be the object of their concern. By allowing them to comfort you, you comfort them, verifying an important process in the lives of others. And you risk returning their love.

## THE GIFT OF GRIEF

The grief journey is painfully long and lonely, but it is not without rewards. You learn that life is not endless and begin to recognize real priorities and goals. You discover greater humility and patience, as grief teaches that there are many things you cannot control and that some wishes go ungratified. You find personal strength and courage to practice acceptance, to meet each day, and to live life.

Grief can open your heart. It asks you to experience a greater depth and range of difficult feelings than you could ever imagine, but it also offers you the chance to experience greater joy. Grief opens your eyes to new perspectives and an appreciation of the beauty in your surroundings. It helps you to distinguish the significant from the trivial, and teaches you how to respond more appropriately to life challenges. It creates a new place for your loved one in your life and heart. Grief moves you to value relationships and let others know how important they are to you. It reflects your capacity to love.

*I learned I could love again. Six years after Jim died, I married a wonderful man and gained three more great children. Together we had six teenagers, and the changes in my life pushed my stress rating off the charts. It was a challenging time for all of us, but my life was enriched. We will celebrate our twenty-sixth anniversary this year.*

*It was from my own problems that I saw the need to reach out to help the bereaved. The knowledge to help others, which I gained from my graduate studies, stimulated my own healing and personal growth. I found a way to coordinate and use my varied interests and talents in ways to make this the most rewarding time of my life.*

# SPECIAL TIMES OF THE YEAR

BIRTHDAYS, ANNIVERSARIES, WEDDINGS, HOLIDAYS, and other times of celebration are difficult for the bereaved. It is important to anticipate these events and prepare yourself to face difficult emotions. You might plan on doing something special to remember your loved one, such as visiting the cemetery, lighting a memorial candle, or sharing memories with other survivors. The following are suggestions for coping:

1) Know that special days will be difficult.

2) Accept that you will likely experience painful feelings.

3) Try to develop new traditions.

4) Share your concerns with others.

5) Ask for support.

6) Trust in and take care of yourself.

7) Count your blessings and find time to help the needy.

8) Allow yourself joy as well as sorrow.

9) Create ways to remember your loved one:

  - Place a wreath at the cemetery.
  - Bring flowers to your place of worship.
  - Make a special toast or request a moment of silence.
  - Spend time with the family album.
  - Encourage others to share memories of your loved one.
  - Give a gift in his or her honor.
  - Buy yourself a present from your loved one.
  - Display a special angel in your home.
  - Plant a tree or a small memory garden.

Honor your loved one during special times of the year. Give others your time and love, and receive the joy and peace that follows.

## Grief Work Exercises

1) Make a list of supportive people you can call and places you can go. Think of ways you can strengthen old relationships and develop new friendships.

2) List the talents or hobbies you once enjoyed. Consider pursuing new interests or a new career. Investigate community resources and sign up for classes that interest you.

3) Write about volunteer positions that might interest you. How would your experiences benefit others?

## JOURNAL

1) List your most lonely times and places. What can you do to make these times and places easier on yourself?

2) Review old needs and expectations and evaluate them for changes. What changes do you see in yourself that you feel good about?

3) Write about the talents you have and how you have used them.

Continue to write in your journal and look back now and then to check your progress. A fresh loss opens old wounds and unfinished business, but sadness does not prevent joy. Allow yourself to celebrate some good times in the light of your sadness.

# FURTHER READING

## GENERAL GRIEF

Borysenko, J. *Minding the Body, Minding the Mind.* New York: Bantam Books, 1987.

Bozworth, A. *Life Is Goodbye . . . Life Is Hello: Grieving Well through All Kinds of Loss.* Minneapolis: CompCare, 1982.

Cambell, A. B. *One to One: Self-Understanding through Journal Writing.* New York: M. Evans and Company, 1977.

Colgrove, M. *How to Survive the Loss of a Love.* New York: Lion Press, 1976.

Fairview Press, ed. *Holiday Hope: Remembering Loved Ones During Special Times of the Year.* Minneapolis: Fairview Press, 1998.

Fitzgerald, H. *The Mourning Handbook: A Complete Guide for the Bereaved.* New York: Simon and Schuster, 1994.

Gaylin, W. *Feelings.* New York: Harper and Row, 1979.

Grollman, E. *Living When a Loved One Has Died.* Boston: Beacon Press, 1977.

Jackson, E. *The Many Faces of Grief.* Nashville, Tenn.: Abingdon, 1972.

Levang, E. *When Men Grieve: Why Men Grieve Differently and How You Can Help.* Minneapolis: Fairview Press, 1998.

Levang, E., and C. Ilse. *Remembering with Love: Messages of Hope for the First Year of Grieving and Beyond.* Minneapolis: Fairview Press, 1992.

Obershaw, R. J. *Cry Until You Laugh: Comforting Guidance for Coping with Grief.* Minneapolis: Fairview Press, 1997.

Rando, T. A. *Grieving: How to Go on Living When Someone You Love Dies.* New York: Bantam Books, 1991.

Tatelbaum, J. *Courage to Grieve.* New York: Harper and Row, 1980.

## CREATIVITY AND SPIRITUAL GROWTH

Capacchione, L. *The Creative Journal.* Athens, Ohio: Ohio University Press, 1989.

Kushner, H. *When Bad Things Happen to Good People.* New York: Avon, 1981.

Montgomery, H., and M. Montgomery. *Beyond Sorrow.* Minneapolis: Montgomery Press, 1977.

Simundson, D. *Hope for All Seasons.* Minneapolis: Augsburg Fortress, 1988.

## LOSS OF A SPOUSE OR PARTNER

Campbell, S., and P. Silverman. *Widower: What Happens When Men Are Left Alone.* New York: Prentice Hall, 1987.

Erickson, S. *Companion through the Darkness.* New York: Harper-Collins, 1993.

Gates, P. *Suddenly Alone.* New York: Harper and Row, 1990.

Ginsburg, G. D. *Widow to Widow: Thoughtful, Practical Ideas for Rebuilding Your Life.* Tucson, Ariz.: Fisher Books, 1999.

Heinlein, S., G. Brumett, and J. E. Tibbals, eds. *When a Lifemate Dies: Stories of Love, Loss, and Healing.* Minneapolis: Fairview Press, 1997.

## ADULT LOSS OF A PARENT

Akner, L. *How to Survive the Loss of a Parent.* New York: William Morrow and Company, 1993.

Brooks, J. *Midlife Orphan.* New York: Berkley Press, 1999.

Commins, P. *Remembering Mother, Finding Myself.* Deerfield Beach, Fla.: Health Communications, 1999.

Klug, R. *When Your Parent Dies.* Minneapolis: Augsburg Fortress, 2001.

Myers, E. *When Parents Die: A Guide for Adults.* New York: Viking, 1986.

## LOSS OF A CHILD

Davis, D. *Empty Cradle, Broken Heart.* Golden, Colo.: Fulcrum, 1999.

Donnally, K. *Recovering from the Loss of a Child.* New York: Macmillan, 1982.

Faldet, R., and K. Fitton, eds. *Our Stories of Miscarriage: Healing with Words.* Minneapolis: Fairview Press, 1997.

Finkbeiner, A. *After the Death of a Child*. Baltimore: Johns Hopkins University Press, 1998.

Ilse, C. *Empty Arms*. Wayzata, Minn.: Wintergreen, 1982.

Schiff, H. *The Bereaved Parent*. New York: Crown Publishers, 1977.

## CHILDREN AND GRIEF

Grollman, E. *Talking about Death: A Dialogue between Parent and Child*. Boston: Beacon Press, 1970.

Heegaard, M. *Coping with Death and Grief*. Minneapolis: Lerner Publications, 1990.

Heegaard, M. *When Someone Very Special Dies*. Minneapolis: Woodland Press, 1988.

Huntley, T. *Helping Children Grieve*. Minneapolis: Augsburg Fortress, 1991.

Wolfelt, A. *Helping Children Cope with Grief*. Muncie, Wis.: Accelerated Development, 1983.

## TEENS AND GRIEF

Grollman, E. *Straight Talk about Death for Teenagers*. Boston: Beacon Press, 1993.

Traisman, S. E. *Fire in My Heart, Ice in My Veins*. Omaha: Centering Corporation, 1982.

## SUICIDE AND MURDER

Carlson, T. *Suicide Survivor Handbook*. Duluth, Minn.: Benline, 1995.

Conrad, B. H. *When a Child Has Been Murdered*. Amityville, N.Y.: Baywood, 1997.

Hewett, J. *After Suicide*. Philadelphia: Westminster Press, 1980.

Lord, J. *No Time for Goodbyes: Coping with Sorrow, Anger, and Injustice after a Tragic Death*. Ventura, Calif.: Pathfinder, 1987.

Smolin, A., and J. Guinan. *Healing after the Suicide of a Loved One*. New York: Fireside, 1993.

## ACKNOWLEDGMENT FOR
## PREVIOUSLY PUBLISHED WORK

"Absence of Place" by Charles Brackbill, first published in *The Cancer Poetry Project: Poems by Cancer Patients and Those Who Love Them*, edited by Karin B. Miller, adapted with permission. "How Adults Can Help Children Cope with Death and Grief" from *When Someone Very Special Dies* by Marge Eaton Heegaard, adapted with permission. "Feeling Person Exercise" from *When Someone Very Special Dies* by Marge Eaton Heegaard, adapted with permission. "Acceptance" and "Letting Go" by Elise L. Hesser, printed with permission. "Trying Times" by Elise L. Hesser, adapted with permission. "Feeling Shunned" from *Remembering with Love: Messages of Hope for the First Year of Grieving and Beyond*, by Elizabeth Levang and Sherokee Isle, printed with permission. "Will I Always Feel Guilty?" from *Beyond Sorrow* by Herb and Mary Montgomery, printed with permission. "Thinking" by Joanna Redman, printed with permission.